SWORN TO FUN!

SWORN TO FUN!

CELEBRATE EVERY
LITTLE THING
TODAY

SCOUT CLOUD LEE, EdD
Survivor Vanuatu Cast Mate

With Carol Ann Washburn Lee, EdD

COUNCIL OAK BOOKS
SAN FRANCISCO / TULSA

Council Oak Books, Tulsa, OK 74104
www.counciloakbooks.com

First edition, first printing

Printed in the United States of America

Cover and interior design by Lightbourne, Inc.

Cover photo by Merrillyn Hartman

ISBN-10: 1-57178-181-1

Library of Congress Cataloging-in-Publication Data

Lee, Scout Cloud.
    Sworn to fun : celebrate every little thing today / Scout
Cloud Lee, with Carol Ann Washburn Lee.— 1st ed.
    p. cm.
    ISBN 1-57178-181-1
    1. Conduct of life—Miscellanea. I. Lee, Annie, Ed. D. II.
Title.
BJ1595.L39 2005
170'.44—dc22   2004027798

THIS BOOK OF PRINCIPLES IS DEDICATED TO our elders, who lived them long enough to prove their worth to us, and to all who have the courage and vision to imagine our world at play. May we gracefully, lovingly, and playfully pass these principles forward to all who have the courage to live a fun life of peace on Earth.

Also by Scout Cloud Lee with Carol Ann Washburn
The Circle Is Sacred: Stalking the Spirit-Powered Life

CONTENTS

ACKNOWLEDGMENTS

KAHLIL GIBRAN SAYS THAT "WORK IS LOVE MADE VISIBLE." This work is made possible because others have given to me the greatest gift: the opportunity to give my gift. Thank you Paulette, Sally, Ja-lene, and Kelly. When you see this work in the hands of our readers, know that together we have shared our love. Annie, you validate me with your every breath and keep me honest. And, of course, I am the lucky one with whom you have chosen to live for the rest of our Earthly lives. Thank you for that anchor.

INTRODUCTION

✺

FOR SOME, LIFE IS A JOURNEY TO THE GRAVE WITH THE intention of arriving safely in a well-preserved, attractive body. Then there are those like me who would rather skid in sideways, wildly waving my hat, body totally used up, tired from hard work, worn out from playin' hard, huffin' and puffin', screamin' "Hell, yeah! Bring it on!"

Life is a one-way trip—eternally! It is all good: the aches and pains, the victories and gains, the lessons and rewards, the easy and the hard. It is what it is, and we may as well be happy about it. Hell, yeah! Bring life on! We're "Sworn to Fun!"

This is pretty much how I live my life. My truth about enlightenment is this:

Be here now, Dude and Dudette.

Now. *This* is it! Search as you might, there isn't anything else. Love it, embrace it, roll with it. Life is a one-way trip eternally on the Up Bus. Get up and stay up. No overs. Meet the moment. Give it your best and highest response, over and over and over again. Find cause for celebration in every little thing, every day.

Cling to principles that you can remember and apply them daily. Remember that principles are basic and fundamental beliefs that have endured the test of time. Here is one of the all-time great ones as spoken by Jesus: "Become again as a child. Believe as a child." Face life bright-eyed and bushy-tailed. The war monger's reality is not my reality. I attract and hang out with others who think as I think, play as I play, work as I work, and feel as I feel. Together we create our own reality. And, the more people we can influence to join our reality, the closer we move to peace on Earth.

I feel strongly that it is the duty of every artist, visionary, and planetary player to send light into the darkness of hearts. We must be beacons of light. Art, music, recreation, dance, and the theater are sister spirits helping to reconnect humanity to our divine Source. We can begin now to give voice to a new vision for our global community. While others may express distaste or fear of the world around us, we must do what we do best: bring people together for the fun of it, the love of it, the joy of it, for peace and prosperity. We must look beyond the bloody aftermath of racial tensions, terrorism, and war that lacerate our communities and destroy our sense of unity. We must look beyond the homeless prophets boxing with their shadows on the street corners. Now is the time to stand on our tiptoes and see hope for our cities and a promise for our children and our children's children's children, for the next seven generations.

The tone set at the beginning of anything determines its destiny. In the beginning was a tone. The sacred breath of God blew as a wind creating a tone, and the tone became light, and the light became all that is. Tone is intent expressed.

Intent programs creation. The tone set at the beginning of a relationship predicts its form. The tone set at the beginning of a project establishes an intent so strongly as to be the best predictor of its success. The tone set in the next few years will etch our future into time. Imagine our world playing together, linked up via satellite, as we create a century where play is a pathway to peace. Planet Earth—Sworn to Fun! The past hundred years granted us time to "oohm" on the mountain tops, run for health, eat every imaginable diet, co-create war, abhor and value diversity, test out the teachings of everyone's guru, scare ourselves with illusions of separation, and then, slowly, to find our way back home. This book of daily principles is a refresher course for those of us who love Cliff Notes, and the lazy person's guide, especially for those who like to "cut to the chase." It is essential reading for tree-climbers, rock-skippers, local and world leaders, all who envision world peace, and any who have ever lain back on a hillside and dissolved a cloud.

The principles in this book have guided my life for over forty years. At first they were a brilliant thought. Sometimes they were thoughts that resonated with my experience. They became notes on my mirror and thoughts for the day. They then became topics for my teachings, knowing that we best teach what we most want and need to learn. Over time, they became more than topics of conversation and debate. They wormed their way into my heart and psyche until one day I looked back to realize that they were living energies in my life. It is my desire that daily practice of these principles will lead others to envision our world at peace, playing together with dignity and respect for all.

The thoughts in this book have drifted into my life and guided me through rapturous enchantment and dark, thundering challenges. For the most part, I don't remember where they came from, how long they stayed, or when they dissolved into living principles. But I have done with them that thing that I know to do with all good things that come my way. I have shared them with others. I've talked about them. I've written about them. I've prayed about them. I've experimented with them. And then, at some point along the way, they became so much a part of me that I have owned them with my love and my life. For all who have said or thought these thoughts before me, I thank you. I may not call your name, but know this: When I say "Thank You, Creator," you, too, are included, as we are all part of the One Great All-That-Is.

I share these living principles as a tribute to all who have lived them. May they prepare us for our reign of peace on Earth. I offer this book as a bridge for us to walk across together toward the light that bonds us forever in friendship. Welcome to my world, where magic is practical, everything is possible, and plenty is ordinary.

Forever Sworn to Fun,
Scout Cloud Lee

"So shall my word be that goes forth from my mouth. It shall not return to me void.

But it shall accomplish what I please. And it shall prosper in the thing for which I sent it."

—Isaiah 55:11

Let it be this way! Amen!
Scout Cloud Lee

JANUARY

A Celebration of Intent...and Little Kittens

I T HAD BEEN A STEAMING HOT SUMMER IN OKLAHOMA, BUT it would soon be followed by a cold, snowy winter. The mice were unusually busy on The Ranch. We decided to get a "barn cat" to help out with the mice. That seems like an ordinary idea to anyone living in the country. However, for us, the idea of making a cat sleep in the barn defies our bent for totally spoiling all our animals. However, we bucked up and firmly planted our intention upon getting a barn cat to deal with the mice.

The want ads listed two locations for free kittens. We arranged to see both litters. Our first stop took us into direct contact with three of the cutest little black kittens on Earth. We couldn't decide, so took all three. The next stop again connected us with three of the cutest little red kittens on Earth.

Again, we couldn't decide and took all three. We arrived back at The Ranch with six little kittens ready to take up residence in the barn.

Our plan seemed immediately foiled when we realized that these little ones would have to endure the bitter winter in the barn. It was with some degree of guilt that we prepared their winter bed, put out food and water and played with them for hours. Then we left them in the barn and went to bed.

We were awakened early the next morning with yowling like none other. We raced to the barn to discover dead kittens scattered everywhere. The one little red kitten who survived came screaming across the yard dragging his back leg. We were horrified. Our young pit bull had found those "strangers" in the barn and proceeded to get rid of them. She got to wear a dead kitten wired to her collar for three days, just long enough to learn never to repeat such an act. Over her fourteen years, she never again dared look at a cat.

By now we were sorely aware that we had gotten way off base from our intent. First of all, the kittens would take a year or more to develop an interest in mice. Secondly, our excess of six versus one came back to haunt us. We intended to get one cat. We ended up with one cat. The surviving red kitten quickly got named "Lion" and was brought inside to heal. He stayed there all winter.

In late spring, we neutered Lion, who was by now quite

spoiled. It would be impossible to describe the look on his face over the whole process. He simply couldn't believe that such a regal being as he had been forced to endure such a process. He took off for a couple of days to protest. Then three, then five, then a week, then two. Soon Lion was gone, only to be sighted every month or so. He would show himself from a distance and let us know that he was still around, but took on all the traits of a truly wild lion. This went on for seven years.

In the eighth year, as the severe winter winds blew in again, Lion began to come closer and yowl and invite our attention. We put food out for him and gradually moved it closer to the barn. It took a full two weeks to coax him into the barn to eat and live. It took another four months to actually touch him.

Today I begin my day by feeding our horses, llama, and donkeys. Then I carry fresh water and food to Lion in the barn, where I climb up on the hay to his nest. There we cuddle and purr and pray together. Many years ago we set an *intent* to have a barn cat to help with the mice. It took almost eight years to see that intent fulfilled. Not a day goes by without Lion and I setting intents together, because he is my strongest teacher of this profound spiritual truth.

Intent is everything. An intent set is a seed planted that will bear harvest in spite of our distractions and detours. The sages of all time know this thing:

Intend well. Project intention into that place that serves divine will and always ask that all be served in the highest possible way.

It's a brand new year. Intend well.

JANUARY 1ST

Anything worth doing well is worth doing really crappy first. Become an eager beginner.

JANUARY 2ND

It's all an experiment. Give life a try. There are no real rights nor wrongs.

JANUARY 3RD

These are the motivating questions: What is going right in my life? What is going so right that I want to grow it?

JANUARY 4TH

What you focus on is what you get. Obstacles are what you see when you take your eyes off the goal. Abandon obstacles! Don't waste your time trying to overcome them.

JANUARY 5TH

Never be swept away by the crowd. Turn and walk into the crowd and know the joy that comes when waves part and allow your passage.

JANUARY 6TH

Don't seek to accumulate. Seek daily to leave something behind. As you do so, you will reach a point of simple vacancy. Into that place will flow your most abundant accomplishment.

JANUARY 7TH

Before a star explodes into the galaxies, it first implodes and gets very, very solid. Sit in the silence. Become solid.

JANUARY 8TH

What you call a problem or weakness is your own soul's attempt to show you your true purpose. If you're scared, you will come to be a model of courage for others. If your knees are weak, you will come to know your true tallness. You will not fear death.

JANUARY 9TH

Relax! God doesn't have time to be bothered with the petty subtleties of your speech and behavior. The silver cord to heaven is *not* attached to your mouth, but rather to your heart's intention.

JANUARY 10TH

Living in the past or future leads to failure. Now is the only accepted time.

JANUARY 11TH

The soul and spirit will grow strong when one learns to pasture freely where few others dare to wander.

JANUARY 12TH

We are magnets for all that is in our lives. We have attracted people and events to us, like bees are attracted to a blossom.

JANUARY 13TH

Duty makes me do things well. Love makes me do them beautifully.

JANUARY 14TH

It doesn't matter how you fall, but how you recover from the fall.

JANUARY 15TH

What we refuse to face and embrace will kill us.

JANUARY 16TH

Wholehearted commitment can only be attached to our ideal. What is our ideal outcome? What are we like at our very best?

JANUARY 17TH

Twice is a pattern. If you observe a behavior twice, know it to be a predictable pattern. Three times is a habit. Four times is a compulsion. Five times is an obsession! Become obsessed with good habits.

JANUARY 18TH

False pride makes one a very big target.

JANUARY 19TH

We are God's experiment with feelings. Express feelings—not ideas!

JANUARY 20TH

Each of us possesses a center. Without our center, we can not tell who we are, where we came from, and where we are going. Seek your center between each breath. Never seek to know another's center. Only your own.

JANUARY 21ST

Where there is a lack of joy, there was a missed opportunity to love.

JANUARY 22ND

When you ask to know your purpose, be prepared to be swallowed up by your destiny. Remembering who you are means submitting to your fate. Trust the powers around to help you.

JANUARY 23RD

Mark my words. If a person's attic is full of garbage, so is his or her mind.

JANUARY 24TH

Be a star. Shine your own light. Follow your own path. Never be afraid of the darkness. When it's really dark, the star shines the brightest.

JANUARY 25TH

When you really want love, you'll have nothing else.

JANUARY 26TH

Reach out and touch what frightens you.

JANUARY 27TH

No gift can come of sacrifice. If you must complain about your gift, don't give it.

January 28th

Ritual is convincing to your unconscious mind. Make a ritual act for all that you intend and want. Your unconscious mind will take you there with no further effort on your part.

January 29th

Don't just talk the story, walk the story.

JANUARY 30TH

Those who attack become what they criticize.

JANUARY 31ST

To know the worth of any dream, dare the dreamer to dirty
her hands building the damned thing. Be famous for having
dirty hands from building the dream of Peace on Earth.

FEBRUARY

Celebrate Letting Go...and Playful Fillies

It was March 7, 1982, when Oklahoma Sunshine Magic came to us. I lay on my belly on the south side of the north pond here on The Ranch. The sun had barely peeked over the horizon when she came. Kanoa had picked the perfect spot for the birth of her second foal. Tahos, the father of this foal, was sired by a Grand Champion American Saddlebred but had been lead-poisoned as a colt. The vet encouraged us to neuter him. He hated the process, and fought it harder than any horse I'd ever seen. We were sure we'd neutered him early enough, so Oklahoma Sunshine Magic was a surprise. She came thirteen months after Tahos was "proud cut."

I lay quietly close by while Kanoa ate the afterbirth and licked Oklahoma to her feet. Already the foal's mane and tail were flaxen blonde and she had a white star on her forehead.

Her coat and mane were curly. She took a few wobbly steps and then turned with full intention and walked directly to me. She stopped short of my face and looked deeply into my eyes. I saw my very soul reflected back through those big brown eyes, and in that moment, I was filled with light and love. I cried from the deepest well of joy. Intuitively, I knew that this was the touch of God's love in me. No church doctrine had ever been able to touch this place. I knew immediately that her name was "Oklahoma Sunshine Magic."

I've had lots of horses, but never one like Oklahoma. I know for sure she loved people more than oats and grain. We "free range" all our livestock on The Ranch, so she followed me everywhere I went. We lay in the sunshine and napped together. She followed me to the garden to pick peas and only ate what she was offered. When I sat on the water troughs, she put her front foot in my lap like a dog wanting to be petted. She even made several attempts to sit in my lap. Wearing a halter and being led was "old hat" to her. She seemed to long for the day that she'd be old enough to carry me, riding free in the wind. I wondered what warrior name I'd give her after our first majestic ride of abandon.

It was the summer after Oklahoma's birth that I left the security of university tenure to strike out on my own. I had only $3,000 in the bank when I decided to go into business on my own. That was hardly enough to pay my bills for the month and left nothing to front a business venture. The decision was a difficult one.

My parents had been living with me while my mother recuperated from her leg injury. I felt responsible for their well-being. I had also believed that I'd only be able to pursue my dreams when there was adequate money in the bank, a belief I defied the evening I decided to leap into the unknown.

It was sunset and I sat rocking on my favorite deck swing. The constant squeak of the swing paced my internal dialogue about the economy. It was lousy. Gas prices were up, jobs were scarce. Folks just didn't have much money. Logically, it seemed like a crazy time to even consider leaving a secure job. Somewhere in the midst of my blithering, I heard my "familiar voice," the one that speaks from my heart. "Embrace your passion. Follow your heart." I decided to visit the bank and study my finances and investments.

It took me two weeks to itemize all my possessions and approximate their value—two weeks and six single-spaced pieces of paper. I had decided to see what I'd be worth if I had to liquidate my assets to survive. Essentially, I was saying good-bye to everything as I checked items off the list. I knew the bottom line: Launching out on my own could cost everything. As I let go of lifetime possessions in my mind, the risk became easier and easier.

My brass bed was a tough one to relinquish, but not nearly

so difficult as Ringo Starr, my 30-year-old paint horse. After several conversations and long rides with him, I was able to add his name to the long list of possible assets to liquidate.

The process was a grueling one for me, but very cleansing. When I finished, I was free to "live my dreams." No fear of loss could stop me. Oklahoma Sunshine Magic's name was the only thing I did not put on my list. She had become the very mirror of my soul, the one thing I had to keep for myself. A woman named Peggy had made that very clear to me. Oklahoma I would keep, no matter what.

Peggy came to The Ranch that June. She was a middle-aged social worker from Chicago. Her body had taken the form of a question mark—stooped shoulders, extended neck, potbellied. I had noticed that body posture on lots of folks who don't normally take risks. She had a lot of questions, but she rarely "lived into" the answers.

"I've never walked a path alone," she told me one day.

"Well, walk!" I replied, pointing to the miles of open countryside. "Pick a path and walk it alone!"

I knew that only by living the metaphor of "walking alone" could she code it into her nervous system and, thus, make it available to her mind. Whatever she was to do uniquely in the universe would require a pattern of walking alone.

Peggy accepted my challenge and turned to embark on the first path she ever intentionally walked alone. She was gone well over an hour. The walk that Peggy took was not just a casual stroll in the woods. Each step was taken without her husband, her children, her friends, her colleagues. She circled out and around the rolling hills of Oklahoma, by the ponds and thickets, and through the dense forest of black jacks and cottonwood trees. She came back to linger in the peach and apple orchard to the north.

The orchard was in full bloom. Newness and sweetness surrounded her. Abundance was the promise of the "walk-alone." She breathed in the aroma of fullness and new life. She stood tall and straight inside the ecstasy of her walk-alone.

"Alone!" The word hit her and reverberated in her ears. "If I walk my path, will I be alone?"

The answer came just in time to stop her tears, a gentle nudge in the back, a surprise visit, a promise! "If you walk your path alone, you'll not be alone." It was Oklahoma Sunshine Magic. She stood waiting for the perfect moment to sneak up behind Peggy. "Surprise! You're not alone!"

Peggy was ecstatic and ran to share her discovery. Then came the second surprise. About a hundred yards down the trail back to The Ranch house, Peggy paused to investigate the "padding" noise behind her. Again, it was Oklahoma, following her.

Peggy flew into my arms with joyful tears rolling down her face. "No one has ever followed me!" she exclaimed.

"Hell, Girl! You ain't been goin' anywhere," came my teasing retort. Peggy's tears and my own all became blurred as I turned to find my wonderful horse and thank her for her gift.

I shall never forget the walk to embrace Oklahoma that day. The wind dried my tears as I strode, tall and straight to the north pasture. My body seemed to lose weight as I glided closer and closer to Oklahoma. She seemed to glow on the hill. Her soft brown eyes fixed on mine once again, piercing my soul. Music was playing like I've never heard before. I was in the music. I *was* the music. That was the first time I know that I heard the angels sing. It would not be my last. I embraced Oklahoma and in so doing embraced the All-That-Is! I embraced the One and the Whole. I embraced all of life.

Oklahoma Sunshine Magic did not go on my list!

November 9, 1982, was a cold, blustery winter night. The wind was blowing hard and long and strong. I lay shivering next to Oklahoma. We were both buried in hay for warmth. For seven days we had battled against a rare virus destined to take her life. For seven days I had cried defiance at any god who would make such a short loan of such a great gift. People from all over North America knew Oklahoma and loved her. She was only eight months old.

A rat that carried the fatal virus had crawled into our local granary and pooped. That grain was packaged up and sold at our local feed store. I brought many sacks of grain home to feed to my nine horses. Oklahoma ate that one fatal piece of grain. A rat and a horse would be my teachers of the greatest lesson of all.

As Oklahoma sucked her dying breath, she spoke through me. "Why?" I cried, and she replied, "Everything, Cloud! Everything! *Cling to nothing!* Your gift must be free of clinging."

As it turned out, the only thing that I was unwilling to let go of in order to follow my dream was the only thing that I lost.

Let go and let God.

FEBRUARY 1ST

To love is to cease all resistance.

FEBRUARY 2ND

When you are in pain, step back on the path of your heart's desire. Follow your passion, no matter what.

FEBRUARY 3RD

Like all of nature, we expand and contract. When we expand, we blend with life. When we contract, we separate from life. Separation hurts.

FEBRUARY 4TH

Conflict never exists between the essence of things. Only between the image of things.

FEBRUARY 5TH

Resist distractions. Ignore those who compare you. Avoid those who speak of limits. Turn from intimidators and impeders. Deny yourself anger. Keep clear your head and your heart.

FEBRUARY 6TH

Understanding truth in the absence of love is like experiencing a telephone call without power.

February 7th

You will only know the love you seek when your roots have grown strong and deep.

February 8th

When you find something good, share it with whomever you can. That way the good will spread out, and who knows how far it will go?

February 9th

Don't eat moths! When you're confused and your mind is in darkness, keep your mouth shut and listen.

February 10th

Always act in order that you might see. Not that you might be seen.

February 11th

Aim at being simple. Simplicity is profound.

February 12th

There is no more sacred place than the place of an old wound filled with love.

FEBRUARY 13TH

The more we love, the faster we vibrate. The faster we vibrate, the slower things feel. As time slows down, we fear less and lose the need to control.

FEBRUARY 14TH

The lovers of your soul are those who want what you have to give.

FEBRUARY 15TH

Bond yourself with those whose eyes reflect back your beauty.

FEBRUARY 16TH

Not until you know that you are truly loyal to yourself can you be loyal to others.

FEBRUARY 17TH

In any task, employ only your hands and your heart. Leave your head vacant to feel the experience of your hands and heart. Then and only then can you say, "I know."

FEBRUARY 18TH

The power is always in the action. Never the declaration of the action.

FEBRUARY 19TH

The best health insurance is a positive attitude and a whole-hearted commitment to do your very best.

FEBRUARY 20TH

Just as a shadow dissolves in light, so does fear dissolve in love.

FEBRUARY 21ST

Know that in "silence" is all knowledge. Seek the silence often. In the silence, meaning is no longer heard, but felt. *Feeling* is the best hearing. Sit in silence and record meaning with your feeling.

February 22nd

When you are off balance, seek the advice of the one who knows you best: Yourself. You are your best coach.

February 23rd

Be mindful of the bullets you send with your thoughts. It is impossible to defend yourself against one of your own bullets returned to you.

February 24th

Your only challenge for the day: Get as many good laughs as you can. Laughter is our greatest bond.

FEBRUARY 25TH

Dream only with focused attention. Never dream with mis-directed thoughts. Misdirected thoughts can kill you. Intend what you will dream at night.

FEBRUARY 26TH

There are many answers already given to you that you have not yet heard. Listen to your heart.

February 27th

It is human weakness to want to be told what to do. Understand this and go beyond it. If someone knew what real wealth was, why the hell would they be trying to talk you out of yours in exchange for advice?

February 28th

What you teach is teaching you.

MARCH

Celebrate Action...and Back Roads

I GREW UP IN A FAMILY THAT LOVED TO TAKE THE BACK roads. There are few things I enjoy doing more than driving down the red, dusty country roads of Oklahoma. Annie and I love to kick back, crank up the country music, roll down the windows, and simply cruise the countryside. Oklahoma is laid out in one-mile squares. Most of the back routes are dusty, gravel roads. The baby green colors of springtime and the miles of winter wheat fields nourish the soul. You can imagine the surprise we felt when, one day we stumbled upon—literally— miles of cattle fence posts topped with cowboy boots.

For as far as you could see in every direction, some ol' farmer who obviously owned lots of land, had collected thousands and thousands of cowboy boots and turned them upside-down on his fence posts. It was beyond our comprehension that someone could own that many boots. We set out to find out how one person could define his borders with boots.

After hours of driving, we arrived at what appeared to be the main ranch house for the Boot Ranch. Only a farmhand was at home. He explained the boot mystery.

His boss had a dream of putting boots on all his fence posts, so he started saving his old boots and those of his family. Pretty soon, friends kicked in their old boots and even bought some from fleas markets and garage sales. Then the word spread to neighbors and on to total strangers. Within a very few years, the old man's land was bordered and cross-fenced with boots. To this day, one can drive north to Logan County and cruise the red, dusty roads of Oklahoma. If you stay with it long enough, you're bound to happen onto the Boot Ranch. Everyone who has ever seen the miles of boots on a fence has returned to add their old boots to the old farmer's collection.

March 4th is a great day to remind ourselves to march forth. If you have a dream, begin. Take action.

Launch, and others will fall in line to support your dream.

MARCH 1ST

Dream both awake and sleeping.

MARCH 2ND

When power comes to you, do not discuss her. Be still with her so as to hold her energy close to you.

MARCH 3RD

You will be a great leader when nothing you own but the joy of giving remains.

MARCH 4TH

Become again as a child with boundless energy and insatiable curiosity.

MARCH 5TH

Without positive and negative poles, there would be no movement. The darkness serves the light. Without it, we would go to sleep and never rise to the challenge of excellence. When the forces of darkness bring us forward to our highest light, their job is done. We pass the test and graduate to the "next," and the forces of darkness move on to other assignments.

MARCH 6TH

Anger blurs the vision and poisons the blood. It is the root of most illnesses.

MARCH 7TH

Consider every relationship an opportunity to give.

MARCH 8TH

It ain't what goes in your mouth that hurts you. It's what comes out of it.

MARCH 9TH

When you wish to express your love, draw your finger along the bones of the face of your beloved so that they may know their beauty.

MARCH 10TH

Be still for an instant and forget everything you have learned.

MARCH 11TH

Grab hold of what opposes you. Don't let it take a toll. Turn this power into something that will benefit the one and the whole.

MARCH 12TH

Choice is a sacred word and our most sacred act.

MARCH 13TH

When you feel grateful in advance of receiving what you want, you are bound to get it.

MARCH 14TH

Compress time. Every second counts for something. The course of our destiny is determined in a moment.

MARCH 15TH

That which knowledge cannot eat up and spit out is a mystery. Hold this mystery sacred. Incessant questions are the mind's way of destroying a mystery.

MARCH 16TH

We come together to repair the damage of forgetting that we all came from the One Mind. Be gentle with yourself and others.

MARCH 17TH

Damn everything but celebration!

MARCH 18TH

Gossip begins behind the hand, but oozes between the fingers.

MARCH 19TH

There is no life without sound. If you want a thought to disappear, take the sound out of it. Poof! Gone! If you want a thought to stay, sing to it.

MARCH 20TH

Through the work of your hands, I can see your heart.

MARCH 21ST

There is nothing more fierce than a woman who can direct her focus.

MARCH 22ND

Stop seeking to be divine. You've already arrived. Relax into being fully human and you'll understand that you are already divine.

MARCH 23RD

Whatever you truly need, you earn, so need never really exists.

March 24th

Never call a disease by name. What we call by name will come running to us.

March 25th

We are servants to our own creations.

March 26th

Collective energy is sufficient to draw water out of the desert. Align yourself and travel in single file. That way your predators may never discern your vast numbers.

MARCH 27TH

What you choose to ignore controls you.

MARCH 28TH

When you make a mistake, name it and claim it. Then fix it.

MARCH 29TH

The only way to access Spirit (all information) is with an open heart. Our rational minds are designed to be servants to our hearts. Open your heart!

MARCH 30TH

We are all made of the same stuff…whatever it is!

MARCH 31ST

Every particle is a living being. Every cell is a tribe of beings. We are all *tribal energy*!

APRIL

Celebrate Desire...and All Surprises

I WAS A YOUNG WOMAN FINISHING MY GRADUATE DEGREES at the University of Georgia in Athens, Georgia. While I competed in many sports and excelled at swimming, I was innately a great runner. What made me great was that I refused to let anyone pass me. When someone got close to me in a race, something went off in my sense of overdrive and I kicked into high gear. I decided to find a coach, train, and go to the Olympic trials in Atlanta. The training went well and actually helped me better focus my work and studies. I was training for the 100-meter dash, in hopes of making it all the way to the 1972 Olympics in Munich.

Daddy was a golfer, so I was familiar with some of the current golf legends. Lee Trevino had written a little book called *How to Succeed*. It was a very simple concept that has since become a natural part of my life. Trevino suggested that we take the time to pinpoint five basic goals for our lives. We were to write them down and post them on our bathroom mirror so we would see them at the beginning and ending of every day. These were my five goals:

1—*Get a Doctorate Degree*

2—*Be Happily Married*

3—*Write and Publish a Book*

4—*Run in the Olympics*

5—*Learn the Art of Having a Gracious Heart*

I posted these goals on my mirror.

At the time, I was deeply in love with the first person who had ever proposed to me. His parents were from India. He had to return to India to tell his parents about me.

They were not happy with his choice and reminded him of his duties as the only son of a traditional family. After six months of harassment, he agreed to marry the girl of their choice. He did not consummate the marriage, returned to America without her, and we began the arduous task of finding a lawyer who could handle a very complex annulment.

The horror of this personal event deterred me from my goal of running in the Olympics. I missed the Olympic trials and, thus, the chance to go to Munich. The terrorist attacks at Munich and the subsequent withdrawal of the USA from the Olympics did little to heal my wounds at the time. Over thirty years passed.

In the fall of 2001, I was down at the barns feeding horses when a UPS truck pulled up to deliver a certified letter. I shuddered to think why anyone would certify a letter to me. With trepidation, I opened the letter only to find the following surprise:

"Congratulations! You have been selected to carry the Olympic Torch in the 2002 Winter Olympic Torch Relay." It went on to explain that someone had submitted my name, and out of hundreds of thousands of applications, I had been selected to carry the Olympic Torch through Oklahoma City. I had only to accept. I burst into tears.

Over thirty years had passed since I wrote down my five life goals. I still displayed my goals in an album, although I knew that running in the Olympics was not a possibility. I had told myself that one unfulfilled life goal would not be a bad average. I had known that I would probably spend a lifetime "learning the art of having a gracious heart." At the time of the invitation, I had gotten my doctorate, written several books, and was happily married to my best friend of 26 years. Here before me was the fulfillment of my fourth life goal.

As it turned out, I ran a lot farther in the Olympics than the original 100 meters.

I had to train about four months to carry a 4-pound weight high in the air while running uphill. The day of the event, January 11, 2002, was not only exhilarating, it was deeply moving. The streets were lined with people waving flags and cheering, and tears of joy rolled down my face as I realized that *God sees our deepest desires and fulfills them in ways we cannot imagine.*

APRIL 1ST

Foolish people look far away for the joy that is so close by.

APRIL 2ND

In the midst of chaos, sit in the silence. Repeat to yourself, "I am empty. I have no resistance."

APRIL 3RD

When people are running away in terror from something, their direction means nothing.

APRIL 4TH

Stretch out and sleep on your belly. It is good for dreaming.

APRIL 5TH

The *tone* set at the beginning divines the end. You can go to the bank on it!

APRIL 6TH

To open our hearts we must love all, beginning with our-selves. Even when we feel no love, love the part of us that feels no love. Love all that we can from wherever we are.

APRIL 7TH

To *do it* is the only way to *know it*.

APRIL 8TH

We are all there is. There is no way to earn enlightenment.

APRIL 9TH

Triumph comes from a whole lot of try and a helluva lot of *umph!*

APRIL 10TH

Learn to look at others rather than pitying or praising yourself. The only true mirror of yourself is reflected in another's face.

APRIL 11TH

Omens are promises, but only if you follow them.

APRIL 12TH

Energy goes where your attention flows. Your thoughts are rivers of energy. Ask each morning, "What will I buy with my attention today?"

APRIL 13TH

It is not the truth we most fear. It is the journey towards truth.

APRIL 14TH

Once you know the way to the center, you visit the place between breaths.

APRIL 15TH

Wallowing is a great waste of vitality.

APRIL 16TH

Judge your lover with your heart, not your eyes.

APRIL 17TH

Constantly needing to say "I am sorry" is an admission of your addiction to guilt and poor planning.

APRIL 18TH

Illness is not caused by anything that passes through the body, but by that which passed through your mind.

APRIL 19TH

Power exists only in the present moment.

APRIL 20TH

View a sunrise as a way of renewing yourself. View the sunset as a way of rewarding yourself.

APRIL 21ST

When you are tired and hungry from hard work, the Provider takes pity on you.

APRIL 22ND

All things break under pressure. Avoid pressure of any kind.

APRIL 23RD

Enlightenment doesn't care how you get there. Just remember that the cameras of life are at the finish line. Slow down. Finish well. And, remember to smile.

APRIL 24TH

When you find a good person, get up early and go be with them. Let your feet never tire of gracing the steps that lead to their door.

APRIL 25TH

Women are the guardians and protectors of our species. When the hearts of women turn to dust, the people will surely perish.

APRIL 26TH

When you live without self-respect, you only imagine yourself to be living.

APRIL 27TH

Know your own heart in solitude where others can't reflect.

APRIL 28TH

You will never get anywhere if your thoughts are watching one thing and your eyes another. Discipline your thoughts to be "here and now." Magic is the ability to focus thought and energy to get results.

APRIL 29TH

Remember the light always flows into darkness. Never does the darkness flow into light. Try it. Open your closet door.

APRIL 30TH

Wholeness and peace is what we *all* deserve.

MAY

Celebrate Humility...and All Teachers

TOM MCBRIDE OF HELENA, MONTANA, HAS BEEN photographer of the year for *National Geographic* several times. Tom was the first person to photograph the mating act of the great golden eagles. He is well respected for his ability to live with and photograph the emotions of wild animals and birds of prey. Tom and I spent the day together on a mountain in Montana, talking about the great teachers in our lives. This is the story Tom told me about his lesson in humility.

Tom wanted to photograph the emotions of the mountain grizzly bears, but it usually took months to get a pass to hike and camp on the mountain tops and rims. Tom struck out without the proper permits to find, live with, and photograph the grizzlies. He was three days into his hike when he realized that a ranger was tracking him. He knew the woman and managed to avoid being caught for another day or two before he finally allowed her to catch up. He confessed his sin of traveling without permits, only to discover that she knew him well enough to know that he basically never got the proper permits. Her true purpose in tracking him was to tell him that grizzly bears had moved into his home at the base of the mountain. He called his home "The Crow's Nest."

Tom shot down the mountain in half the time it took him to climb it and arrived back at The Crow's Nest to find a mother bear and two cubs having their way in his home. He waited until they left for the day, then carefully roped off the porch and kitchen area with string and tiny bells. His plan was to rig his cameras in the dining room with enough flood lighting to photograph the mama bear at night. The bells would alert him to her presence. That evening Tom waited with buckets of ice water and his cameras.

He wanted to photograph a look of "Surprise" on the face of a mama bear.

Somewhere in the early hours of the morning, Tom was awakened by the tinkling of bells and movement of bears. He crept into position. When the mama bear was close enough, Tom flipped on the lights and cameras and flung a bucket of ice cold water directly into the face of the bear. To Tom's amazement, the mother bear did not flinch. Only feet away, she stared at and through him. The ice cold water ran down her face and onto her chest. She remained unmoving, staring. Expressionless. Slowly Tom began to back away from the bear. Surely she must have been thinking, "Tom, you wanted to photograph grizzles. So here I am. I came with my kids to help you out and you throw water in my face." Rather than photographing "shock" or "surprise," Tom learned his greatest lesson in humility. In his own words, Tom said, "Never have I felt so vulnerable, so humble." Gratefully, the bear and her cubs left and Tom restored order in his house. *Let us stand humbly before the Great Giver of our Breath, knowing that at all times God sees us...sees through us.*

May 1st

Be friendly toward what is new and it will quickly make peace with you.

May 2nd

The plants can get along without us. We cannot get along without them. Pay them proper respect.

May 3rd

Withdraw your trust in the strength of weapons and put your trust in the strength of God.

MAY 4TH

When a thought that weighs you down comes marching through your mind, abandon the thought. When you turn your back on it, it will pop like a bubble. It can only take form if you turn your attention to it. Some thoughts are worth attending to.

MAY 5TH

Personal desire is the true force behind manifestation.

MAY 6TH

Truth never compels. It leaves the choice open for you to act freely.

MAY 7TH

Those who truly love do their best and forgive the rest…beginning with themselves.

MAY 8TH

When you sit in one place repeating "Thanks," you deny yourself expansion. Once is enough!

MAY 9TH

"To abandon" is a strong act. It means turning your back, with no intention of returning…as to "abandon smoking." To "live with abandon" is also a strong act. It is the direction you are going once you've turned your back and walked away.

MAY 10TH

We never really change what we see, only the way we see it. We must hold attention on what seems ugly until it becomes beautiful to us. Otherwise, we simply feel indifferent to it.

MAY 11TH

Who cares if you are right? Are you happy? Is it possible for me to be dead wrong in your eyes, and yet very happy?

MAY 12TH

Fear seems to signal withdrawal, when, in fact, we've already withdrawn too far. "All forward" is the command. Life is a river trip.

May 13th

If something breaks and falls away, let it go. The beauty lies within.

May 14th

Our most necessary medicine is wildness. Anything that grows wild is stronger than that which is tame. A handful of wild onions carries more flavor than a bushel of tame ones.

May 15th

We must learn to live simply so that others may simply live.

MAY 16TH

Strength comes from pruning.

MAY 17TH

Believe as a child. Receive as a child. Only then will you know the Kingdom of God within.

MAY 18TH

Grief will never propel you forward. Only joy.

MAY 19TH

When you ask for my opinion, be willing to sign a contract releasing me from your disappointment in your life thereafter.

MAY 20TH

When you waiver, you can not expect to receive.

MAY 21ST

Nothing can be imagined that is not out there. Take your imagination seriously. Own your thoughts and act toward them with respect. When you refuse to accept the reality of your thoughts, you refuse to accept yourself, and that will bring pain.

MAY 22ND

When faced with a long journey, focus on the process.

MAY 23RD

Whoever speaks the softest wins the argument.

MAY 24TH

No task is so important that it can't be laid aside to give love to those who come seeking.

MAY 25TH

See the Messiah in the face of every child.

MAY 26TH

All thoughts are living entities. Like people, they have to live their lives and receive a proper burial. Each thought you create feeds on you until it is laid to rest. When you ignore a thought, it becomes like a tick on a dog, feasting on your life blood. However, if you abandon a thought forever, it will starve to death, like all things that don't get fed.

MAY 27TH

Know three things: fearlessness, nonresistance, and love.

May 28th

The trophy for the race does not necessarily belong to the fastest runner, but rather to the one who just keeps right on running.

May 29th

No cause justifies fear; no work motivated by fear contributes to a better world.

May 30th

Sing from the heart so the Great Spirit can feel if what you want to say is true.

MAY 31st

When others are giving you directions, listen with your strong eye focused firmly on your own outcome. If what they have to say enhances your outcome, you'll know it. It will have a holding place. If it doesn't, it will pass without deterring you from your course.

JUNE

Celebrate Appreciation...and Little Churches

PAWNEE, OKLAHOMA, IS THE HEADQUARTERS FOR THE Pawnee Indian Tribe. Near the center of town stands a small Indian church regularly attended by about eighteen people. Among the small congregation is an old traditional Indian woman who only speaks her mother tongue. Few remaining Pawnees remember the old language.

Each Sunday, one of the church families would take the little old woman home with them for dinner. She had no family of her own. As months went by, the congregation began to whisper to each other about their experience with the old woman.

Each Sunday she would quietly eat with different families and then spend a couple of hours sitting on the porch or in the living room while family visited and children played. The old woman never talked. When it came time for her to leave, she would take the hands of her hosts and say something strange in her native tongue. The hosts, not knowing what she was saying, would smile, nod, and then take her home. Always she said the same thing and everyone wondered what it meant.

One day an old uncle came to visit from Taos, New Mexico. He joined the little old woman on the Sunday visit for dinner. The hosts were delighted to discover that the uncle spoke the old language and was able to converse with the old woman. As always before leaving, she took the hands of her hosts and uttered her same expression of gratitude, but on this day everyone knew they would finally learn the meaning of her speech.

"What did she say?" they asked the uncle.

He smiled and told them, "She said, 'I feel better about myself having spent this precious time with all of you.'"

What greater gift is there than this: to come away from any experience saying, *"I now feel better about myself due to your kindness"*? Let this be the feeling of all who cross our paths in life.

JUNE 1ST

Politeness requires a period of silence.

JUNE 2ND

Without flesh, God has no feelings. We are the great heart of God.

JUNE 3RD

This planet is not about pure thought. It is about pure feelings.

JUNE 4TH

All things have a place. They like to sleep in their own bed. Return things always to where you found them. Keep your house in order always expecting Spirit to arrive at any moment.

JUNE 5TH

You will never get anywhere if your thoughts are watching one thing and your eyes another. Discipline your thoughts to "be here now."

JUNE 6TH

When someone says to you, "This is the way," it ain't!

JUNE 7TH

Many trails will cross and diverge on your journey. But to reach your true destination, choose one trail and stay on it.

JUNE 8TH

Carry no crosses that hump your back. Know your true tallness.

JUNE 9TH

Your soul is a child. Act in your body to keep your soul happy.

JUNE 10TH

Don't look back. God's got the back door covered.

JUNE 11TH

When warriors are faced with odds that can't be dealt with, they retreat and play!

JUNE 12TH

Everything has a mouth and must be fed, including your thoughts. Find the proper food for your thoughts. If you want to flow, drink water. Some thoughts should be starved immediately.

JUNE 13TH

The effort required to obliterate anything, in fact, grows it.

JUNE 14TH

When you soften your eyes, I can hear you better.

JUNE 15TH

We may have love without peace, but never peace without love. "Love one another," says the Prince of Peace.

JUNE 16TH

Love is to expand. It is the energy that embraces the unloving.

JUNE 17TH

Shit left unstirred soon quits stinking!

JUNE 18TH

The true addictions: guilt, pain, fear, remorse, and anger.

June 19th

Not a single person could fail if all people had at least one other who saw them as successful.

June 20th

Put things back where you found them. Pick up after yourself. Leave every space nicer than you found it. Deal with your own garbage so that you never have to deal with the garbage of someone else.

June 21st

Since you have two ears and only one mouth, cultivate the habit of listening twice and speaking once.

JUNE 22ND

Effortless peak performance is the magnificent outcome of wholehearted commitment. Magic follows commitment.

JUNE 23RD

Our health is linked to our ability to manage our responsibilities. Become responsible for all your thoughts and actions.

JUNE 24TH

Remember, when you stand in the light you can never get rid of your own shadow. Embrace your shadow.

JUNE 25TH

When you want to help a person with his burden, make light of it. It will lighten his load.

JUNE 26TH

Life's humbling experiences call forth the magnificence of one's own pride.

JUNE 27TH

When you stop the flow, disaster occurs. Consider our rivers.

JUNE 28TH

Avoid doing the impossible. It takes too long!

JUNE 29TH

A wise person will look twice at each thing to make certain that she sees truth.

JUNE 30TH

You can only "own" what you recognize with your heart and care for with your life.

JULY

Celebrate Surrender...and the Rattlesnake

M Y FRIEND BROOKE IS CROW. SHE INVITED ME TO HELP the Cauldwells round up their cattle from the Little Big Horn on the Crow Reservation. On our trip out to Montana we noticed an unusual number of bears. When we arrived at our base camp, we were startled to find a cow with her head knocked half off by the single swat of a very large bear. It was rumored that some bears from Yellowstone had been released into the Little Big Horn.

My mount for our three-day round-up was a very large red-and-white paint who soon gained my deep respect for his sure-footedness. He was head shy and cautious, while possessing amazing strength and endurance. I assumed that someone had beaten him around the head, so I vowed to gently gain his trust. At the time I didn't know how important that decision would be.

Our mission was to round up 400 head of cattle from the mountains and bring them down to base camp. It took a couple of long days of riding to locate most of the cattle.

Well into the first day, we realized how right we had been about the prevalence of bears. Berries were stripped, logs clawed for ants, and trails were dotted with bear droppings. Several times a day we would sight a bear in the distance. Needless to say, we were cautious and constantly singing to alert the bears of our presence. We definitely did not want to surprise a bear or get caught in an aspen grove with one. We knew that the bears could outrun our mounts.

Near the end of the third day, we had succeeded in collecting almost all the herd and were working them back toward our base camp, which sat at the end of a long mountain draw. I was riding at the back of the herd when a lone cow decided to turn up the side of the canyon wall and head to an aspen grove topside of the draw. Knowing that my mount was very sure-footed, I decided to race ahead, cut up a rocky canyon trail, and get between the cow and the grove. We all wanted to avoid the chance of meeting up with a bear in that aspen grove.

The plan was working until my mount and I lunged up over the top of the canyon trail only to land in a very active rattlesnake pit. My horse's hooves came down with a thud in the middle of a community of rattlesnakes standing at full attention and rattling to beat the band. I found myself thrown into a heightened state of awareness, simultaneously terrorized and deeply peaceful. My horse froze where he stood, statuesque, not moving a muscle. I melted into his body and we became one. In this moment I totally understood what it meant to surrender.

A silent voice spoke out to the rattlesnakes from our One Heart. "Oops! We apologize for landing in your living room. Please grant us peaceful passage."

An eternity passed in those few seconds, and then the largest snake of all came down from his point and slowly slithered backward. He must have been the chief because all the surrounding snakes followed his lead. The path they left was no more than five feet wide. With the greatest of dignity and aplomb, ole' Sure Foot walked from that pit in the slowest of "slow motion." It was as if he was on Quaaludes! I remained unmoving, one with my mount.

When he cleared the pit, he tucked his tail and leapt from harm's way.

It is well known that horses are terrified of snakes and will typically explode in their presence. On this day, that sure-footed red-and-white paint horse earned a life of leisure with me on our ranch in Oklahoma. We named him Sedona Sure Foot and brought him home where he has lived for the past twenty years.

Sedona has learned to trust us and he has earned the title of "Professor" here on The Ranch. It is Professor Sedona Sure

Foot who leads the young colts on all their early trail rides and teaches them patience, trust, and surrender to our touch. Sedona Sure Foot saved my life and taught me the *power of surrender*.

JULY 1ST

Listen with your eyes closed so you can truly see.

JULY 2ND

Passionate desire has a way of vacuuming your soul. Old hurts fall away.

JULY 3RD

This beautiful Earth Mother has a body and a soul. She is alive and sensitive. Treat her with respect.

JULY 4TH

"Stand up!" is a command. "Stand tall!" is an invitation.

JULY 5TH

Strength and beauty lie at the center. Go to the core of things. Go deep.

JULY 6TH

When you speak, keep your heart in front of your ass.

JULY 7TH

When you are troubled, you are stepping into a calm stream. Be still and see that the stream will soon flow unclouded again.

JULY 8TH

We need everything that happens to us. Embrace it. Love it. Let it go.

JULY 9TH

If you must yap, at least let it flush the birds into flight!

July 10th

Never say to God, "Prove Yourself to me." It is our job to prove God.

July 11th

The more you awaken, the more you are response-able.

July 12th

Any problem I am having is my own. I must be willing to bring it to the altar and alter my mindset about it.

JULY 13TH

Pride comes right before you hit the ground.

JULY 14TH

The good in service has little to do with the service itself. It has to do with the heart one brings to the service. An unwilling heart spoils an act by infecting it with the feelings of resentment and anger. Choose to do or not to do. Then, bring forth a willing heart.

JULY 15TH

The truth is this: There is really a surplus of what we need.

July 16th

We stand tall in the presence of all life's lessons.

July 17th

What you are looking at is exactly where your body is taking you. What do you see in your mind's eye? Your body is the willing servant of your mind.

July 18th

When you strike a child, you imprint mischief. When you rebuke a child in public, you harden the child's heart.

July 19th

What you recognize, you own. What you own, you give importance. Ownership has nothing to do with money.

July 20th

God did not divide into six billion parts. God multiplied into six billion parts. We are all God.

July 21st

Be willing to be made up of the wildness of you.

JULY 22ND

All your days of not having can prove you have everything.

JULY 23RD

Command this of God: "Make me wise and brave."

JULY 24TH

A sacred marriage is the bonding of the power that courts you.

JULY 25TH

When you fail, it is because you thought you would.

JULY 26TH

True power is never in the point that you make, but in holding absolute control of yourself.

JULY 27TH

The straight path belongs to one who will travel from warmth to cold and back again.

JULY 28TH

War is never outside ourselves. It is always from within.

JULY 29TH

Protection is toxic to the person being protected. You are your own best guardian of yourself.

JULY 30TH

Sleep when it is necessary. Eat when it is necessary. Too much of either makes us vulnerable and dulls our perceiving power.

JULY 31ST

Avoid speculations and wonderings. Live your questions.

AUGUST

Celebrate Respect...and All Brothers

BEAR HEART WILLIAMS IS A RESPECTED ROAD MAN, HOLY
man, and teacher among the Creek nation. He lives in
Albuquerque, New Mexico. I met Bear Heart years ago and
learned to call him "Uncle." It is with great respect for him that
I share his personal story of respect.

As a young boy, Bear Heart experienced the deep and
abiding love between his grandfather and his grandmother. He
still remembers the great sadness and loneliness his grandfather
experienced when his grandmother died. Many months after
losing his wife and life partner, Bear Heart's grandfather heard
a knock on the front door. He opened the door to find the old
town drunk unsteadily standing before him dressed in a crum-
pled Sunday suit. The old drunk had sobered up as much as he
could, gone to the Salvation Army and bought an old suit,

cleaned up, and come to visit with Bear Heart's grandfather.

Years before, Bear Heart's grandfather had adopted the old man as his brother. At the time, the man was not a drunk. However, life had been hard for him, especially when he lost his wife and children in an accident. Bear Heart's grandfather had always been a brother/friend to the old man, even after he became the town drunk. On this day, the old drunk returned the kindness.

As he stood before Bear Heart's grandfather, he said, "Brother, I have come to sit with you. You see, I know what it is like to return home after a hard day at work and be greeted at the door by the same smiling woman who married me years before. Now you return home to silence. I know what it is like to sit in my favorite chair and glance into the kitchen to see my wife of many years cooking me my favorite meal, and now you stare into an empty room. I know what it is like to awaken from a deep sleep in the middle of the night with my arms around the same woman who has warmed me for a lifetime, and now you reach and feel empty space. I know about your loss, my brother. I am here to sit with you."

In that moment Bear Heart saw his grandfather make the gesture of deepest respect: He knelt down, touched the feet of the old drunk and said, "Thank you, my brother. Come and sit with me."

Let us respect All-That-Is!

AUGUST 1ST

When you desire to do God's will, remember that your will is God's will.

AUGUST 2ND

Giving increases what you possess.

AUGUST 3RD

All the while you watch, someone watches you. Life is not a dress rehearsal. We are always on stage. Always.

August 4th

Where there is defensiveness, the mind has identified an illusion.

August 5th

When you go "crying for a vision," you will get sympathy. When you come "commanding" a vision, you get a vision.

August 6th

When someone is just plain rude to you, shrug it off. It's a burden for them to carry around. Not you.

AUGUST 7TH

Make amends for injuries to others. Balance a bad deed with a good deed in the present.

AUGUST 8TH

Learn with a spirit of "go!" not "whoa!"

AUGUST 9TH

To speak without story or rhyme lulls us into the dull world of sanity.

AUGUST 10TH

Violence is a poor survival strategy.

AUGUST 11TH

Hurry and worry…worry and hurry. A fast pace going backward. It almost always wastes time to hurry, and it wastes life to worry.

AUGUST 12TH

God is love. Love is God!

AUGUST 13TH

Never, never, never, never, *never* harbor a negative thought. That's the best advice I know about. Think about what you want. Not what you don't want. What do you want?

AUGUST 14TH

Never stop owning yourself…not even for an instant.

AUGUST 15TH

God is sworn to fun. Morose worship bores even God.

AUGUST 16TH

It is not human nature to think the very worst. It is shear slothfulness.

AUGUST 17TH

Truth is what works.

AUGUST 18TH

The only difficult requirement: Throw away harsh thoughts.

AUGUST 19TH

Peace means being loyal to oneself. Loyalty bridges the gap between thought, talk, and action.

AUGUST 20TH

All fear murders something.

AUGUST 21ST

What is imagined will be carried out in minute detail. Be careful what you imagine.

AUGUST 22ND

There is only one way to success. Live life your own damned way!

AUGUST 23RD

Water is the most powerful Earth energy. It is completely nonresistant.

AUGUST 24TH

Listen always with your heart.

AUGUST 25TH

A good scare is better than the best advice.

AUGUST 26TH

Sleep with your attention devoted to your own purpose.

AUGUST 27TH

Public chiding turns one against the other and causes resentment to grow.

August 28th

What you put out is what you get back. Put out a happy tune and happy singers will join your trip.

August 29th

Give to nothing that is a struggle.

August 30th

The journey you make is a one-way eternal trip. Never look back. Only forward.

AUGUST 31ST

Walk quietly among the many as though your life depends on it. It does.

SEPTEMBER

Celebrate Each Thing Having a Place...and Daddies Everywhere

MY DADDY WAS A MAN OF VERY FEW WORDS AND LOTS of laughter. He giggled at almost everything, especially life's drama. When we would "have a fit and fall in it," Papa would just giggle. His IQ was high and his words were few. Perhaps there is wisdom in this. He basically felt that others' business was none of his. Thus, when Papa coached me about something other than sports, I listened. One of his strongest lessons had to do with orderliness.

Just the other day, a young woman was proclaiming all men to be babies who throw their clothes around and generally leave messes everywhere. I simply had to share with her the experience of my daddy. Papa folded his own laundry and put it neatly in his dresser drawer. He always safety-pinned his socks together when they were not on his feet. He never put a toilet seat up or left one up. He had a place for everything and believed that everything had a place. "Put things back where you got them," he would say. A hammer is a hammer only if it can be found and used as such. Otherwise, it's just rusty junk laying out in the yard." He would explain to us kids: "A tool has a place, just like you have your own bed. If you use the hammer and then put it back to bed, it can be used again by the next guy. How would you like to be thrown out in the yard to sleep?"

Papa had a point. To live in communities or families, we must learn to share tools and property in a way that all can have access. An orderly house and tool shop is likened to an orderly mind. Clarity of thought is likened to clarity of space. I often suggest to people whose minds are boggled with junk thoughts that they go clean out their attics. Your environment is a reflection of your mind. To this day, I won't rent one of our apartments to a person who has a junky car. I know absolutely that they will keep house the same way.

Papa taught a few others lessons about life through his carpentry philosophy.

"If you're going to use a wheelbarrow, it's best to turn it the direction that you'll be going before you fill it up." Life is so much easier when we keep our minds and houses in order, put things back where we got them, and *turn in the direction we want to go before filling up our minds and our space.*

SEPTEMBER 1ST

The words you speak become a pied piper in search of resonance. When your words arrive back at your door-step, they will have multiplied many-fold.

SEPTEMBER 2ND

Act not that you might be seen. Act that you might see.

SEPTEMBER 3RD

Treasures belong to those who first see them.

SEPTEMBER 4TH

Excuses are boring and rob you of your power.

SEPTEMBER 5TH

Sworn to fun is better than sworn to none!

SEPTEMBER 6TH

Where your eyes look, your body will follow.

SEPTEMBER 7TH

Never marvel at one who kills, only at one who heals. Turn off those kids' cartoons.

SEPTEMBER 8TH

People who are always waiting gain weight.

SEPTEMBER 9TH

A question is an answer on the way.

SEPTEMBER 10TH

Loosen up! A tight body is addicted to its own negative emotions.

SEPTEMBER 11TH

Learning is not so important. Knowing is.

SEPTEMBER 12TH

You can only receive what you can see yourself receiving.

SEPTEMBER 13TH

Real heroes never fight for money, glory, or promotions.

SEPTEMBER 14TH

Any medicine object is only as good as the eye and the heart behind it.

SEPTEMBER 15TH

In times of trouble and of great joy, remember this: There is always a balancing out. Always, there is a balancing out.

SEPTEMBER 16TH

A man sings to the sky. A woman sings to the Earth.

SEPTEMBER 17TH

A woman holds and nurtures the dream of life. A man champions and powers the dream of life. A child dreams the dream of life. Know this balance within yourself and you will always walk your dream path and always attract to you the proper support for that dream.

SEPTEMBER 18TH

When you live as the Great Provider intends, you will surely discover your true inheritance.

SEPTEMBER 19TH

You can only own that which you recognize for its beauty and care for with devotion. When you look away from what you say you "own," someone will take it from you.

SEPTEMBER 20TH

Never teach with force of any kind. Rather, teach with gentleness and patience.

SEPTEMBER 21ST

When you walk this Earth, wherever you put your feet, the powers in the ground and in the Earth are yours to use. Use them, or they will use you.

SEPTEMBER 22ND

You will be a good leader when you own nothing but the joy of giving.

SEPTEMBER 23RD

When you require knowledge, a teacher will always appear. Keep your eyes and heart open. Teachers come in all shapes and sizes.

SEPTEMBER 24TH

Know this: There is a place provided in the tribe for every manner of person and every disposition.

SEPTEMBER 25TH

Some say, "What would you want me to know?" The wise say, "This is what I will to know."

SEPTEMBER 26TH

Don't tell others how to live. Just share with them the spirit of your own life.

SEPTEMBER 27TH

When people ask me, "What is your lineage?" I say courage…lots of courage.

SEPTEMBER 28TH

A moment of vision is worth a lifetime of darkness.

SEPTEMBER 29TH

If you follow your heart path, you'll always be safe.

SEPTEMBER 30TH

Abandon the lodge of self-pity and don't ever look back.

OCTOBER

Celebrate Feelings...and All the Courage It Takes to Embrace Them

AS A YOUNG WOMAN IN GRADUATE SCHOOL AT THE University of Georgia, I attended my first big concert. Ike and Tina Turner were performing at the coliseum, and I had seats at the top of the top of the building. I went armed with a pair of binoculars.

Tina was fantastic. She was wild and energetic. I was spellbound with her amazing talent. In those days, Ike and Tina had a hit song called "What You See Is What You Get." I took those words to heart. Over the next 30 years, I developed a philosophy that promoted "visioning all that we want." As the book says, "As a man thinks, so he is." I carefully outlined my goals and made collages of my dreams. I taught others to do the same. I built models of what I wanted to manifest.

In time, much of what I wanted to manifest came to me, always in a different form than I "saw." This spawned some level of disappointment. Much of the time, while I waited for the arrival of my "vision," I suffered from impatience and often sat on my pity pot, whining about how much I deserved my vision, wondering, "Why aren't things happening faster?"

Gratefully, I grew through these agonizing years and came to understand the power of emotions. I came to understand that it is our *feelings* that create the resonating core into which flows manifestation. I came to understand that the form in which our desires will manifest is often best left to our Creator. I learned that if I could feel the experience of having the thing I wanted, I could manifest it more quickly. I also learned that what was manifested most often far exceeded my wildest expectations. I began teaching this newfound wisdom.

Recently, we were in a long security line at the Tulsa International Airport, awaiting our flight to Las Vegas. Standing in front of us was a black man dressed in a white suit. I looked twice to discover that the man was Ike Turner. We were wild with excitement. I told him of the years I had been inspired by his and Tina's song "What You See Is What You Get." The song goes on to say, "What You Don't See Is Better Yet." Ike and I began singing the song together.

To my surprise, when we got to the line about "what you don't see is better yet," Ike stopped me to say, "I've changed the lyrics to this. He then sang the new lyrics: "What you see is what you get...what you *feel* is better yet!" I almost kissed his feet for the affirmation of a lesson that took me thirty years to learn. *Let us celebrate our feelings and learn to FEEL all victories even before the game.*

OCTOBER 1ST

All things grow in a circle. The circle is sacred. It focuses all attention on the center. Always meet in a circle.

OCTOBER 2ND

Learn to see with your "strong eye." Reach into the mystery of all things and bring the information immediately to your heart. Let your heart take the information to your head so that you can truly "see." Then, and only then, will you speak the truth.

OCTOBER 3RD

Don't point. Tilt your chin or cast your eyes in the direction that you wish to draw attention.

OCTOBER 4TH

It is good sometimes to stare at the moon till you lose your senses.

OCTOBER 5TH

It is not what goes into your mouth that defiles you, it is what comes out.

OCTOBER 6TH

To live the beautiful way is to see the inherent truth that underlies all great religions.

OCTOBER 7TH

It is our spiritual duty to be happy. A happy child always has something to give — a toy, a song, a candy bar. Even the poorest household always has enough in the pot to feed a welcome guest. Be happy. Spread a sense of merriment wherever you go.

OCTOBER 8TH

An empty feeling always comes when you've lost something that you love. The only way around it is not to love anything…and then you feel empty all the time.

OCTOBER 9TH

When you don't know how far you are going, it's always far away.

OCTOBER 10TH

When people are afraid, tell then to sing real loud. Distract their conscious minds and they'll be able to make it to the top of the mountain.

OCTOBER 11TH

When we are born, we choose to put our spirit minds into a body to test the spirit and make it stronger. That's why birthing always causes such a ruckus. The spirit is bucking, getting back into a body and taking exams.

OCTOBER 12TH

Things got messed up when women started following to be with men. The reverse should happen. A man should follow to be with a woman. She holds in her belly the only hope of life.

OCTOBER 13TH

We must learn to be one body…one heart beating. Little streams come together to make the great rivers.

OCTOBER 14TH

When you hold your words in, you will lose power. Hold in only those things that would bring sorrow before its time.

OCTOBER 15TH

It is only from a very high mountain that all the rivers can be seen running to the sea. Look for me on the mountain.

OCTOBER 16TH

As a leader, think always of the good of the people, speak calm words to those in troubled times. Use your seeing power to "see" ahead of the next moon.

OCTOBER 17TH

Storms are Mother Nature's way of pruning and clearing. The same is true of life.

OCTOBER 18TH

The wind shows you which way energy is moving. It's best to get in the flow.

October 19th

It is best to fish and pick berries in the spring and summer. Leave the hunting till fall and winter. Spring and summer are mating time for the animals because nobody can mate and fight for life at the same time.

October 20th

Birds are always a sign of something. A laughing owl lets you know that a big change is coming. Crows are blabber mouths and let you know where danger is. House wrens bring good luck when they move into your house. Hummingbirds bring protection for living on the edge. Eagles and hawks bring messages of hope back to you. Whippoorwills are a sign of good dreaming. Red cardinals mean that you'll get money. Turtle doves bring love messages from far away.

OCTOBER 21ST

When people giggle, they look younger.

OCTOBER 22ND

Things that grow underground should be planted by the dark of the moon. Things that grow above ground should be planted by the light of the moon.

OCTOBER 23RD

When people give public testimony about their sins, it always causes trouble.

OCTOBER 24TH

In just about all things you have two chances—one against the other. Some people hesitate and say, "What if I fail?" The real question is, "What if I don't?"

OCTOBER 25TH

When you travel, ride beside your thoughts. Never let them get away from you.

OCTOBER 26TH

Silence is the voice of the Provider. It must be felt with the heart, rather than heard with the ears.

OCTOBER 27TH

Open to receive. Let there be no struggle.

OCTOBER 28TH

Choosing is your most important act on Earth.

OCTOBER 29TH

Life force will not direct or compel you…you direct it. Stop waiting around for the "rescue."

OCTOBER 30TH

Grab hold of what opposes you and turn this power into something that you want…something that will benefit the one and the whole.

OCTOBER 31ST

Honey, if you want to pierce your nose and color your hair purple, do it. Just make sure to keep a smile on your face so you won't scare people.

NOVEMBER

Celebrate Persistence...and All Who Just Won't Quit

NOVEMBER IS MY BIRTHDAY MONTH. NO ONE THING IS AS important to my success in life as persistence. My father used to say, "Sister, you can do anything you want to do if you'll just stick with it long enough." My grandfather was named Grover Cleveland Spencer. I never knew Papa's father. For this reason, I created my own special grandpa hero out of Grover Cleveland Spencer. It was fueled by my daddy's stories about his father.

According to Papa, my grandfather owned a dry goods store in Ft. Myers, Florida. It was called The Popular Price Department Store. It was the only one in Ft. Myers at the time. Everyone in town shopped there. Because of this, my Grandfather knew Thomas Edison and Henry Ford, both of whom wintered in Ft. Myers. Henry Ford told my grandfather a story that he passed down to my daddy.

Apparently, Henry Ford had his challenges in starting up the automobile industry.

To begin with, he had to convince people that they needed a car at a time when there were really no streets for them and very limited fuel outlets. Developing a sales team to sell an expensive "tough buy" product had its own special challenges. Henry Ford had finally gotten a team of 25 young salesmen together and was sharing sales facts with them. Typically, a salesman has to be able to endure hearing "no" twenty-five times for every "yes." Henry Ford then told the young men that "they could do anything if they would just stick with it long enough."

One young man stood to his feet to object. "Mr. Ford, I beg to differ. You see, for as long as I might wish to carry water in a sieve, I can never do so." Henry Ford paused for a moment and then replied, "Son, if you are patient enough to wait until winter, the water will freeze and you'll be able to carry that water in your sieve."

Papa used this story to coach me to completion and success for the span of his lifetime. We now know that *persistence* is the most quoted key to success. *You can figure out how to do anything you want to do if you'll just stick with it long enough.*

NOVEMBER 1ST

Get rid of everything that is not necessary.

NOVEMBER 2ND

We grow in compassion when we lose the need to destroy the beliefs of others.

NOVEMBER 3RD

Everything must have a sense of worth. Give even your hound dog a duty he can succeed at.

NOVEMBER 4TH

Some people pretend to love things that they can't understand. That just can't be done. If you've got a love, then you've got an understanding.

NOVEMBER 5TH

Be the method, don't teach it.

NOVEMBER 6TH

Don't be afraid of this Earth walk. We're only here for a visit. The Earth walk is a dream born of an even greater dream.

NOVEMBER 7TH

When you learn to be alone, you will cease striving. Be alone in any crowd.

NOVEMBER 8TH

Live your questions. When you hear a question mark at the end of a sentence, expect and prepare to be living the answer.

NOVEMBER 9TH

Dream walker will never lull you into boredom. Stay always alert in the classroom of your dreams.

NOVEMBER 10TH

Who is stronger: prey or predator? The hunter can choose states of attention without risking his life. The hunted must always hunt the hunter. When you are preyed upon, know that you are in training as a huntress or hunter.

NOVEMBER 11TH

When people call you crazy, bless them. They have granted you the freedom to do as you damned well please.

NOVEMBER 12TH

When faced with a survival situation, hang "tuff!" Hang loose!

NOVEMBER 13TH

It seems the older you get the more you tend to forget the bad in things…so I guess the bad doesn't count anyway.

NOVEMBER 14TH

The night darkness dies really easily, while the day leaves slowly. It's a good thing to remember in the hard times.

NOVEMBER 15TH

A busy hand helps the angry head forget.

November 16th

In truth, one can not sell the Earth any more than they can sell the sky in four directions. The Earth owns herself. We are her caretakers.

November 17th

People only sit around with their mouth full of talk when their hands are empty.

November 18th

Dress in a neat way. Wear the amulets of your heart's passion and the colors of your people. This way you show respect to the Great Spirit.

NOVEMBER 19TH

One who denies his power for winning weakens the spirit of the game he enters.

NOVEMBER 20TH

It seems to me that most doctors prescribe drugs of which they know very little, for diseases about which they know even less, to people about whom they know absolutely nothing. The "medicine way" is simply the craft of keeping people amused while nature takes her course.

NOVEMBER 21ST

Dare to be authentically…naturally…Y-O-U!

NOVEMBER 22ND

No true friend will do for you what you are able to do for yourself. To try to learn what others know is to distract yourself from really acting upon your own memory. We already have everything we need inside of us. We are here to grow into ourselves.

NOVEMBER 23RD

Enlightenment = Chop wood, carry water, make fire, and keep your mouth shut!

NOVEMBER 24TH

The ground beneath us is always moving as are the stars on which our course was first mapped. Learn to hold a firm focus and have a good recovery strategy for the shifts that are bound to come.

NOVEMBER 25TH

Share your best, chuck the rest.

NOVEMBER 26TH

Look to yourself for leadership.

NOVEMBER 27TH

Rekindle your inner light with boundless loving.

NOVEMBER 28TH

You can catch a turkey if you can trick him into falling into a hole. He could hop out, but he doesn't. A turkey is like some people. Since he thinks he knows everything, he won't ever look down to see what's around him. He's got his head stuck way too high in the air to learn anything.

NOVEMBER 29TH

Life should not be a journey to the grave with the intention of arriving safely in an attractive and well-preserved body. I want to skid in sideways, Champagne in one hand, strawberries in the other, body thoroughly used up, totally worn out, and screaming, "*Woo-hoo! What a ride!*"

NOVEMBER 30TH

The answer to every question: "Open your heart!"

DECEMBER

Celebrate Completion...and Peace on Earth

MARK IS A PSYCHIATRIST BROTHER/FRIEND OF MINE. HE IS fun, and funny, and quite the adventurer. Years ago, he decided to take a vacation to Spain to see the traditional bull fighting. He went alone with a pass for seven major fights. This is the story Mark relates about his experience.

The first fight was shocking. Mark is a peaceful man. He is an animal lover. He waited with bated breath to see the beautiful dance between man and beast. The arena gate opened and out ran the bull. The first bull ran hither and yon, up and back, over and across. The crowd roared. Another gate opened and out came a picador clad in pink. He attracted the bull with his cape, flashed it back and forth, and watched as the bull threw his head from side to side. Several times he narrowly slipped away from the deadly horns. Then the picador began driving swords into the neck muscles of the bull, three on one side and three on the other. With the jab of each sword, the bull dropped his head lower and lower. The crowd roared with each lunge and plunge of the sword. When, at last, the bull charged with his head held low and steady, the crowd bellowed for the matador.

Another gate opened and out walked the stately matador adorned in red. The crowd roared again and again. Now began the dance. The matador teased and challenged the bull to charge, and the bull did. The crowd roared again and Mark marveled at their enthusiasm. When the crowd bellowed one final roar, the matador drove his sword deep into the heart of the bull, killing him with one lunge. Mark nearly choked.

Fight after fight, day after day, Mark watched the event with growing sadness and remorse at his plight. He had so wanted this vacation in Spain, and now he longed to run far away from this arena of death. The picadors and the matadors and the crowd seemed insane to him. His heart went out to the innocence of the bulls being slaughtered. Mark decided to forfeit his last ticket and return to the good ol' USA. However, Mark is a man committed to completion. Mark stayed for the last fight.

On this day, the crowd called for the bull to be released into the arena. This bull would be like no other. The gate opened and the bull ran headlong into the center of the arena and stood poised toward his fate. His head was unmoving. The crowd went wild.

To Mark's surprise, the picadors were called off and the gate opened to allow the matador to enter the arena. He walked toward the bull undaunted by imminent danger. The matador stood poised before the bull, red cape in hand. He shook it lightly and the bull charged straight toward the cape. The matador moved it only enough to avoid direct contact with the bull. Again and again the bull charged straight ahead at the matador, his head steady, his focus sure. And repeatedly, the matador danced to the side, with the bull sliding right beside him. Mark had never seen such excitement. People around him cried with delight and awe. Mark was witnessing a dance of death between man and beast...a dance that held both to supreme precision. The dance was beautiful and fully intimate.

Suddenly, the crowd exploded with applause. The dance was over and the beast was spared his life. The crowd had called for the bull to be saved and retired to a pasture of plenty and pleasure. The matador and his bull would go down in history.

Typically, a bull would approach his death with defiance and erratic behavior. The picador's job was to steady the head of the bull for the fight with the matador.

After the kill, the crowd would call for certain body parts to be awarded to the matador for his performance—an ear, two ears, a hoof, or more, and sometimes a tail. However, on this day, when the bull faced his hour of death with focus and precision, the picadors were called off. Mark discovered that this dance between bull and matador was the most coveted performance in the life of a matador. The true reward was in being given the bull to procreate future bulls of courage and valor. Had Mark left before the last fight, he would never have fully understood the true tradition of bullfighting.

Each day may we strive to complete what we begin. May we face our destiny with courage, focus, and stillness. *May we intimately dance with Spirit.*

And, may we know the true power of Peace and pass it on to all future generations.

DECEMBER 1ST

Don't talk about Peace. Make Peace. Begin at home.

DECEMBER 2ND

There is no peace on Earth without peace of mind.

DECEMBER 3RD

We are a part of "The Grand Experiment" on Earth. Here, we experience our thoughts through a physical body. What we think and feel, we live.

DECEMBER 4TH

We are "One" with the Creative Force. We have taken on physical form to walk among, admire, and nurture our own collective creation. This Earth is the physical manifestation of our collective "intent."

DECEMBER 5TH

We must awaken to ourselves as the Creative Force. What is in our lives today came at our beck and call. Sometimes our beck and call is our resistance. What we resist, we also energize.

DECEMBER 6TH

We are beings of Light that influence the quality of our rivers, our seas, our winds, and the growth of little children.

DECEMBER 7TH

We are intended to communicate through simple thought with all things. We have only to think of a friend across the miles to immediately "see" them and know from the "seeing" how they are. Trust this "seeing."

DECEMBER 8TH

We are fearless souls who know how to adjust when we understand that change is the only constant in our lives.

DECEMBER 9TH

We are natural leaders and true friends when we recognize the unique specialties in others.

December 10th

Our lives are intended to reflect the magnificence and wonder of a curious child entranced with continual imagination and awe.

December 11th

Let us be the people who come believing, trusting, and dreaming awake our potential, so that all can awaken.

December 12th

Our creative essence is that of totally fun-loving, pure, courageous, curious, and loving children, intent on playing all day, all night, dreaming awake our intended reality of beauty. We are all children together. It's OK to play!

December 13th

Life on this Earth plane is a "game" planned by ourselves in the beginning as part of the "One Mind." We then decided to conduct a little experiment, just for fun. "Gee," we thought, "what would happen if we gave ourselves physical form too?" We thought into material form the beauty of this Earth and then wanted to put ourselves inside our own creation. Through our collective creative thought, we created a paradise and then allowed ourselves to walk among our own thoughts. We continue to do the same today. We have only to look at the world around us to see our own creations. We are not "playing God." We are One with God.

December 14th

Our challenge is to find a way to "remember" our beginnings and awaken ourselves to the truth of our Oneness with All That Is. Until we do so, we sleep outside the Great Circle. We must awaken to our Creativity and join the dance.

December 15th

We hold in our hands the possibility of a World Celebration. The finest and noblest intent of every human being is for Peace of Mind, Peace of Spirit, and Peace on Earth.

December 16th

We yearn for Peace in the same way we yearn for clear air, clean water, nourishing food, comfortable shelter, loving friendships, inspiring ideas and ideals, healthy relationships, and happy children.

December 17th

Peace is not just a principle. It is life in action. It's a state of being. One day, governments will have to get out of our way and follow us to Peace.

DECEMBER 18TH

We drill, coach, and reward our children for competition. What would happen if we coached, drilled, and rewarded cooperation? Peace! Peace would happen!

DECEMBER 19TH

Please.......No more war toys.......Please!

DECEMBER 20TH

Is there a picture more beautiful than our tiny blue planet hanging in space, obviously so alive? We must care for Her. Really, really care for Her.

December 21st

It is our privilege and responsibility to save and nurture all future generations, all animals, and all plants. The tiny butterflies, the exotic flowers, and the colorful fish of the sea are all in our keeping.

December 22nd

Animals supposedly, without reason, live in a state of social amity. They herd together, flock together, feed together, care for each other, raise their young together, and even come together to consult about migration patterns. "Coming Together" is a law of Love that takes place throughout all of nature. What of human beings?

DECEMBER 23RD

When we truly love ourselves and our sweet Mother Nature, we will know Peace on Earth.

DECEMBER 24TH

We belong to this Mother Earth. We must stay close to Her or we will become very lost. Bless those who have retained a wildness of nature.

DECEMBER 25TH

Inside each one of us is a knowing that we must do something important. We may not know what it is, but we must be always ready to take advantage of the opportunity when we get our chance.

December 26th

Our words go marching forth and exert influence on all and everything around us. Our deeds flow from our heads, our hearts, and our hands, and are made visible for years to come.

December 27th

When our peace is not shaken by others, or by fear, or by anger, or by excitement, it is truly *peace*.

December 28th

Blessed are the Peacemakers for through each of us, we will have our sweet Mother Earth for our children to inherit.

December 30th

Dear God, please talk to all the warring people of the world. They don't know what they are doing. Grownups just can't be trusted with guns, and bombs, and titles that let them push people around.

December 31st

We need everything that happens to us. Embrace it. Love it. Let it go.

*Planet Earth, **Sworn To FUN**: Families Uniting
Neighborhoods, Friendship Uniting Nations.*

PRAYERS
AND
SONGS

THE LORD'S PRAYER:

THE PRAYER OF JESUS
Translated Directly from Old Aramaic

Giver of my breath, moving through all things, giving all of creation heart and soul....

Soften the ground of my being, making always in me a place for Your Presence. Let my bones be hollow so that Your Spirit can flow freely through me. In my deepest place, plant Your seeds with greening power, so that I might be both midwife and husband to all of Creation. Let me move to the heartbeat of Your great purpose. With passion and soul, let me grow from within all that is needed to live each day fully. Help me untie the tangled knots of my destiny that would bind me to past mistakes, and turn me from all that would divert me from my true course. Allow me to enlarge the opportunities of each moment. Let me be the ground of Your fruitful vision, the birthing power and the fulfillment of Your heart's desire. In this way, all is made whole again.

A Ho! and Amen!

SCOUT'S PRAYER OF
THANKSGIVING AND PEACE

I am Scout, and I clasp hands with each one of you and send my words to your ears from my heart. Thank you for being here to experience the power of One Heart Speaking.

PRAYER: Precious Creator. Great Provider. Giver of Our Breath. We praise your creatures and all of your creation. We speak with gratitude for your immense Love that brings us into direct relationship with all things. We show our obedience to your Divine Law by our respect for You, The Great "All That Is."

We stand together with the Great One, Our Brother/ Friend Jesus, and acknowledge His act of Love that grants us this intimate audience at Your Throne. We follow His directions Home....We "Come believing as little children." We open ourselves to being lead into our future by our children. We adore The Child within our own hearts and all others.

Thank you for seeing our good intentions here and knowing about our devotion for our children out seven generations. Thank you for blessing our Children. Thank you for forgiving us when we are off the mark, and for standing us back on the path of the sacred arrow to the heart of things. Thank you for forgiving us as we are willing to forgive ourselves and each other. Thank you for letting our heads be small enough to wear the many hats that are passed to us each day. Thank you for letting our feet fit easily into the moccasins of all our relations who walk this Star Path Home to Peace on Earth.

Thank you for standing us tall in the presence of both friends and enemies. Thank you for helping us hold back our tongues when our words would speak imbalance. Thank you for helping us speak always to spin the sacred spiral that brings together all things in perfect harmony and peace.

Thank you for keeping strong the sweet aroma of our heart's fire burning, until that day when we finish our work here on Earth and You call us home to the Great Council Fire. We stand center of Your Presence, which is far more precious than all of your Many Names. We command the giving of our gifts to be the vehicle for Your Miracles here on Earth.

Spirit Divine, flowing always through us....we are Your Family on Earth.

We are many nations. Together we have spoken on behalf of all children out seven generations. We Stand Inside our Visions and Experience of Peace on Earth.

A Ho! and Amen!

Spirit's Time Has Come

A SONG BY CLOUD

Sons and Daughters of the Stars. Tribal Members of the Great Central Sun. Sisters and Brothers of the Entire Intergalactic Federation.....Know this to be true!!! *Spirit's time has come!*

Giver of our Breath! Great, Great Spirit! We speak with gratitude for the *love* that brings us into direct relationship with all things.

Walk on...with Spirit by our side. Walk on…with Spirit as our Guide. We hold *all* hearts within our hands. We trust ourselves and make a stand. When we dare, we know we can! ...Spirit's time has Come!

Our intentions are good and our devotion is deep for our children out seven generations! When we're off the mark, we know to step back on the path of our heart's desire. We command our feet to fit easily into the moccasins of all our relations that walk the Star Path Home.

We stand tall in the presence of all life's lessons. We hold back our tongues when our words would bring imbalance. We speak always to spin the sacred spiral that brings together all things in perfect harmony.

Keep strong the sweet aroma of our heart's fire burning.

Great Spirit...we stand center in your Presence, which is far more precious than all of your many names. We command miracles here on Earth with the giving of our gifts. We see your wisdom etched in the lines of ancient elders prayin' power. We hear your love songs in the wind and see your smile in every flower. We feel your *happiness* in the waves of island palm trees dancin' wild! And hold your love of simple things in the hands of every child!

Walk on! Walk on! Spirit lives inside! Walk on! Walk on! SPIRIT is our Guide. We hold All hearts within our hands. We trust in LOVE and make a stand. When we dare, we know we can. Spirit's *time has come! Spirit's time has come! Spirit's time has come.*

Please join us in a dream.

WE BELIEVE THAT EVEN ONE MOMENT OF PEACE, FELT world wide, would shift our global consciousness. For twenty years, we have promoted the vision of a 24-hour WORLD PARTY with simultaneous activities experienced worldwide. As the old song says, "What would happen if everyone lit just one little candle? What a bright world this would be!" We now possess the technology to link up our world and choreograph a celebration of life on our planet. Imagine drumming together, singing together, praying together, toasting together, planting trees together, dancing together, and saying "Thank You" together. Imagine beginning the day in Vanuatu with drums bringing up the sun. Imagine following the sun around our world for a day, stopping to celebrate some simultaneous event along the way. If we could only experience "togetherness" on our planet once, we would shift our consciousness toward Peace on Earth. Then truly we would understand *Sworn to FUN*: Families Uniting Neighborhoods and Friendship Uniting Nations. Wouldn't it be **FUN**, just for a day, to **Celebrate Every Little Thing?**

We celebrate you and thank you for reading our book.

Scout and Annie

Scout and Annie Lee

DR. SCOUT CLOUD LEE

Scout is an inspirational and motivational entertainer. The spirited wisdom, tenacity, and integrity she displayed as a *Survivor: Vanuatu* cast mate, earned her the role of tribal leader. Scout is a speaker, author, storyteller, corporate executive and corporate trainer, songwriter, singer, musician, and artist. She has survived divorce, bankruptcy, artificial knee replacements and terminal cancer.

Former tenured professor at the University of Illinois and Oklahoma State University, Scout has been awarded numerous federal grants for her research in peak performance and human excellence. She is the author of eleven books and hundreds of articles on these subjects and has been featured on documentaries and television specials by all major television networks.

Currently CEO of Vision Us. Inc., an organization- and team-development firm, Scout is internationally renowned for a communication technology known as "The Excellence Principle," and corporate training programs called "The Challenge of Excellence" and "Tracking Peak Performance." Some of her steady clients include The United States Postal Service, The Federal Aviation Administration, The Department of Transportation, Ford Motor Company, Kimberly-Clark, The Chickasaw Nation, and The Institute for Management Studies. Her broad appeal extends from keynoting IBM International and corporate training in Washington, D.C. to writing and performing music globally.

DR. CAROL ANN WASHBURN LEE (ANNIE)

In 1980 Annie joined with Scout to create "The Challenge of Excellence," an experientially based training program designed for corporations. Annie also established a highly successful training base in San Diego, California, where her company received national and international acclaim. She then expanded experiential learning technologies to Kaua'i, Hawai'i. While immersing herself in the rich culture of Hawai'i she researched the communication challenges and gifts inherent in diversity. In addition to continuing her consulting business, she headed the funding campaign for a local non-profit to successfully build a cultural community center after the devastation of Kaua'i by Hurricane Iniki.

In addition to *Sworn to Fun! Celebrate Every Little Thing* **Scout and Annie** co-authored *The Circle is Sacred: Stalking the Spirit-Powered Life* (ISBN: 1-57178-136-6, Council Oak Books, $17.95), which presents ancient wisdom and contemporary spirituality as vital parts of everyday life.